PHALLIC THIMBLES

THE ILLUSTRATED BOOK OF SEXUAL TRIVIA

DAVID SMITH AND MIKE GORDON

Firebird Books

FOREPLAY

Graffiti spotted on a wall in California, following his success in the movie "10", claimed that Dudley Moore was not so much a phallic symbol as a phallic thimble. Not that this worries Dudley Moore; it's common knowledge that the very best surprises come in small packages!

Graffiti like this seems to prove the point: sex continues to fascinate us despite being among the most basic and regular of human activities. The truth is that when it comes to other people's sex lives, everything is trivial. When you are involved, nothing is trivial. Sophia Loren claimed that, "Sex appeal is 50% what you've got and 50% what people think you've got". It was easy for Sophia to say this, for in her case the ratio is more like 80:20.

The topic is perennial. In 1971, British singer Tonia Berg said: "Sex is like money — very nice to have but rather vulgar to talk about." Nevertheless, in the following pages, you'll find a miscellany of sexual trifles described by David Smith and illustrated in Mike Gordon's humorous and apposite cartoons. The sexual habits and oddities of kings and commoners portrayed show that nothing really changes over the millennia.

The fact that Napoleon's penis was bought by an American urologist for $3800 may seem trivial to you — but it was probably important to Napoleon. Luckily, it happened after he was dead! Yet, triviality is not what it seems. The original application of the word "trivial" was the study of grammar, rhetoric and logic in Medieval universities. So, you can see that important people have always studied such matters. Read on, be educated and amused — you may end up thinking like Mae West: "I used to be Snow White," she said, "but I drifted".

WELL I NEVER!

The women of Northern Siberia are reputed to show their affection towards men by throwing slugs at them.

Gandhi slept with naked women in order to test his celibacy!

All the members of the '20,000 Club' have had sex in an aircraft at more than 20,000 ft (6,080m).

In France there are towns called 'Condom' and 'Arsy'.

Until the twentieth century, Egyptian men preferred not to deflower their brides. Instead, they generally paid a servant to do it for them.

The only female competitor who did not have to undergo a sex test at the 1976 Montreal Olympics was HRH Princess Anne.

There are at least 500 slang words in the English language to describe the penis.

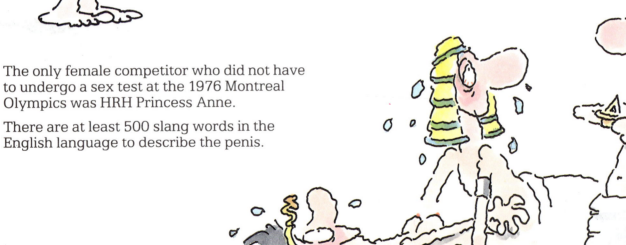

The oldest sex manuals were published some 5000 years ago in ancient China.

One doctor from the USA claims to have used hypnosis to enlarge the breasts of his female patients.

More than 10 million vasectomies are performed each year throughout the world. A case of 'to have and have not'.

Pope John XII was beaten to death by a frenzied husband in the year 963 when he found the pontiff making love to his wife.

At least three women — one each from Australia, Great Britain and the USA — maintain that they have been raped by creatures from outer space.

Brigham Young, the Mormon leader, was the father of 56 children.

'Intercourse' and 'Climax' are names of towns in the state of Pennsylvania, USA.

The 'grey itch' is slang for the male menopause.

Anorgasmi is the inability to have an orgasm.

In Jamaica, the male sex organ is often referred to as a 'teapot'.

The name of the Grand Tetons mountain range in Wyoming, USA, means literally 'Big Tits'.

Mrs Ida Maitland of Great Britain was reputed to have had a bust measurement of 152 inches (386cm).

It wasn't unusual for British men in Victorian times to tie string round their genitals at night to prevent nocturnal emissions.

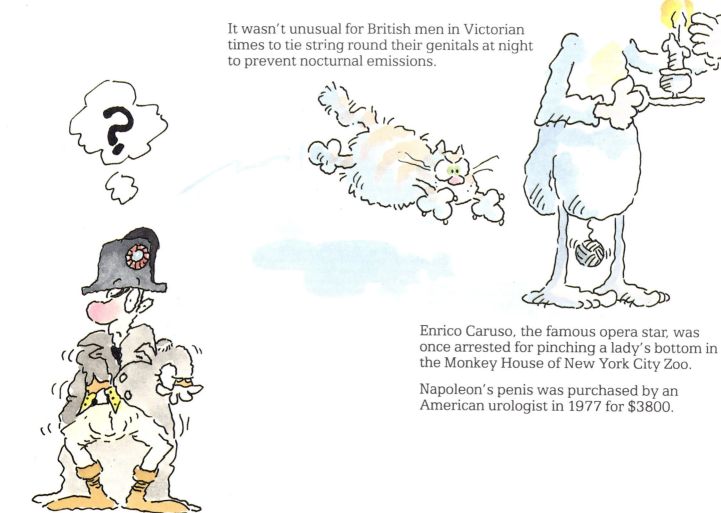

Enrico Caruso, the famous opera star, was once arrested for pinching a lady's bottom in the Monkey House of New York City Zoo.

Napoleon's penis was purchased by an American urologist in 1977 for $3800.

Benjamin Franklin, the American statesman and scientist, became a member of the exclusive Hellfire Club in 1735 and helped to organise elaborate orgies for the members.

Adulterous women were dealt with severely when King Canute (1016–1035) was on the throne of England – they had their ears and noses cut off. It is not recorded what happened to adulterous husbands!

THERE'S NOT MUCH THAT'S NEW

Casanova, born 2 April 1725, was a multiple seducer. He had two favourite contraceptive devices — a sheath made from a sheep's intestine, and a half-lemon used as a Dutch cap. Because of his activities, he almost married his own daughter! Luckily, the girl's mother appeared at the ceremony just in time for him to recognise her as a former lover and the marriage was called off.

Catherine de Medici had a hole drilled in her bedroom floor so that she could watch her husband enjoying sex with his mistress in the room below.

The Marquis de Sade's mother was a nun. He was notorious for his sexual perversions and cruelty from which the term 'sadism' is derived.

Madame de Pompadour really tried her best to retain the love of King Louis XV of France, and to this end she lived on a regular diet of truffles, celery and vanilla — supposedly very effective aphrodisiacs.

Lady Emma Hamilton (1765–1815), the mistress of Admiral Lord Nelson, was once a London prostitute. Also, she was employed as a 'goddess of health' by a quack doctor when she danced in the nude around a 'celestial bed'. This particular therapy was supposed to cure childless couples' infertility.

Cesare Borgia (1475–1507) was the unscrupulous son of Pope Alexander VI. His wedding night was virtually ruined by a practical joker who substituted laxatives for his normal medication.

In 1657, Prince de Condé, a French general, achieved his all consuming ambition – to make love twelve times in a single night! To commemorate this remarkable achievement he had all his shirts, buttons, cuff-links and all accessories marked with the number 12.

Marie Antoinette and King Louis XVI of France didn't consummate their marriage until seven years after their wedding – a novel version of the seven year itch.

SEVEN ENERGETIC LOVERS

King Solomon. He ruled Israel for forty years (973–933 B.C.) during which he had 700 wives and countless mistresses.

Cleopatra (69–30 B.C.). She took her first lover when she was 12 and from then on, the Queen of the Nile, used sex for power as well as pleasure. She retained scores of male lovers with whom she perfomed the erotic mysteries she had mastered in a bordello in Alexandria.

Sarah Bernhardt, the French actress, had more than one thousand lovers in her vibrant life of 79 years.

King Ibn-Saud (1880–1953). This Saudi-Arabian monarch began his sexual activities when he was 11 years old. He enjoyed sex with three different women each night until he died at the age of 72.

Catherine the Great (1729–1796). Sexually, very, very greedy; the Empress of Russia advocated sexual relations six times a day. It is *certain* that she had 21 lovers, but it is suggested that she had at least 80.

Lola Montez (1817–1861). When she was only 13 years old, the British-Irish dancer realised that she could sell her body for money. She had three husbands and many lovers, including Franz Liszt, the composer. Eventually she became the mistress of King Louis I of Bavaria. It is claimed that the king said of Lola: 'She can perform miracles with the muscles of her private parts and caused me to attain ten climaxes in one day'.

At one time the King of Tonga was required to deflower every virgin on his island. At the age of 80 he was still carrying out his duties several times a week.

THEY WERE FIRST

First Sex change operation, performed by Dr Karl Hamburger in 1952 when G.I. George Jorgensen, underwent surgery at the Serum Institute, Copenhagen, Denmark and became Christine Jorgensen.

First State controlled brothels requiring registration and the inspection of prostitutes were introduced in France in 1778.

First Birth control clinic was opened at 46 Amboy Street, Brooklyn, New York on 16 October 1916 by Margaret Sanger.

First Rhythm method of birth control was devised by Dr Herman Knaus of Berlin in 1928. It was approved by the Vatican in 1930.

First Contraceptive sheath or condom is attributed to Gabriel Fallopius, Professor of Anatomy, Padua University, Italy, in 1564. The sheaths, made of linen, were tried out by 1100 different men.

First Vaginal cap or pessary was produced by Dr Friedrich Wilde of Berlin. It was the first use of rubber for 'surgical goods'.

First Oral contraceptive – the pill – was produced by Dr Gregory Pincus of USA in 1954. The first commercially produced oral contraceptive was Enovid 10, marketed by G. D. Searle Drug Co of Illinois, in August 1960.

First Syphilis outbreak in Europe was in Barcelona, Spain, following the return of Christopher Columbus from the New World in March 1493.

First Striptease (other than the Biblical exploits of Salome) took place at the Four Arts Ball, held in Paris in February 1893. Mona, an artist's model, stripped for the benefit of the students and was fined 100 Francs, which provoked a full-scale riot in the Latin Quarter.

First Nude calendar was produced in 1913. The picture, a study of a girl standing ankle deep in a lake, was a reproduction of a painting by Paul Chabas.

First Silicon breast implant was devised by the Dow Corning Corporation, Midland, Michigan, in 1962.

First Human artificial insemination was carried out by M. Thouret of Paris University. He made an intravaginal injection of sperm on his sterile wife in 1785 which resulted in the birth of a healthy baby.

MARRIAGE FACT FILE

The first marriage partners to be selected by computer were Shirley Sanders and Robert Kardell, both 26 years of age. They were married at the First Presbyterian Church, Hollywood, California, in October 1958.

A wedding announcement in 1963 appeared in England in *The Times* – the marriage of a Mr Cock and a Miss Prick.

The first wedding performed in an aeroplane in flight took place on 31 May, 1919, when Marjorie Dumont married Lt. S. W. Meade in a Handley Page bomber at 2000ft (608m) over Houston, Texas.

Hymen was the Greek god of marriage.

The world's most wedded couple married for the first time in July 1937. Since that time, Edna and Jack Moran of Seattle, Washington, have repeated the ceremony more than forty times.

Ann Hayward and Arno Rudolphi were the first couple to be married whilst making a parachute jump on August 25, 1940, at the New York World's Fair.

SPIRITUAL NICETIES

Until about 1890, castration kept Vatican choirboys singing sweetly.

It was only in 1123 that the Roman Catholic clergy adopted the practice of celibacy.

Priestesses in ancient Indian temples used to have sex for money with male worshippers — all proceeds went into the temple treasury.

Pope John XII made a rather unorthodox use of the Basilica of St John Lateran — as a brothel.

It's a special blessing for an Orthodox Jew to have sex on a Friday night.

In 1484, Pope Innocent VIII became known as 'The Honest' when he admitted that he did have illegitimate children.

STATISTICALLY SPEAKING

In western society, 53% of women prefer men on top during intercourse.

According to *Playboy* magazine, more women than men use pornography as a sexual stimulant.

During her reproductive years the average woman has intercourse 3000 times.

According to the renowned sexologists, Masters and Johnson, one in four men are impotent by the age of 65. However, other research informs us that 73% of all men are still potent by the age of 70. It looks as if we shall just have to wait and see!

A *Sunday Times* survey revealed that 40% of women find a man's buttocks to be the most admirable part of his body.

According to recent research, the average time for a woman to reach orgasm is 11 minutes.

Some 72% of all men in Western countries use a condom for birth control on their first encounter.

Apparently, three million Italian couples make love in motor cars because they have nowhere else to go.

A world-wide survery of men's tastes in women disclosed that plump women were more in demand than slim ones.

In the USA 13% of men would like to have sex more than once a day.

A Royal Commission of 1863 in the UK reported that in Scotland almost 90% of women were pregnant on their wedding day.

Anita Loos was proved right. A 1986 survey confirmed that 68% of American men DO prefer blondes.

It seems that 45% of American men prefer to make love with the lights on – this is rather unfortunate as only 17% of their women favour it that way.

Ladies may find it useful to learn that scientists have confirmed that male sex hormones are at their peak in the autumn and winter.

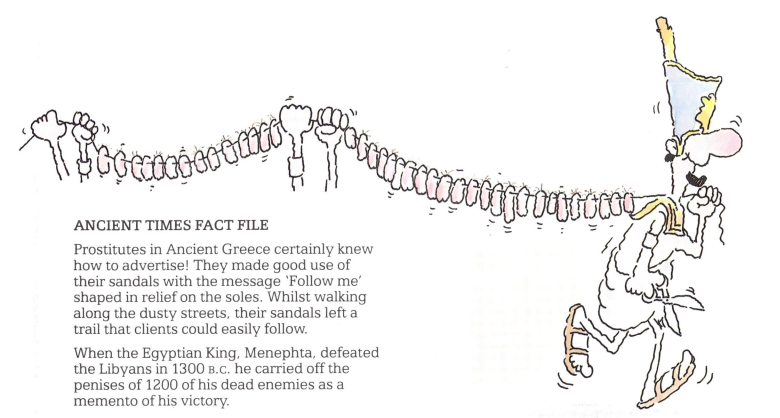

ANCIENT TIMES FACT FILE

Prostitutes in Ancient Greece certainly knew how to advertise! They made good use of their sandals with the message 'Follow me' shaped in relief on the soles. Whilst walking along the dusty streets, their sandals left a trail that clients could easily follow.

When the Egyptian King, Menephta, defeated the Libyans in 1300 B.C. he carried off the penises of 1200 of his dead enemies as a memento of his victory.

Women of Ancient Greece had an interesting birth control technique – they held their breath, squatted and wheezed!

It was customary for men of Ancient Rome to place their right hand on their testicles when taking an oath.

It is said that the first international chain of brothels was established by the Romans.

Women of Ancient Rome wore a *mamillare* to support their breasts – the original bra?

PROSEX DEVICES

There seem to have been many ingenious devices developed for the enhancement of sexual pleasure.

Protective coat
The shrinking of the penis in chilly weather can be most disconcerting to the owner. To counter this, an open-ended moulded tube of plastic insulated by foam rubber is worn. This appliance was patented in 1964.

Penis support
This vital aid was invented in 1968. A tube of high quality flexible plastic, leather or rubber is placed around the penis to induce stiffness and to provide support. Another advantage is claimed by the inventor — it's a help in countering a limp penis during insertion.

Breast-developing jacket
This extraordinary aid, granted a patent in 1970, has surely resulted in increased bust measurements for innumerable women. The jacket is linked, via flexible pipes, to a convenient hot water supply which flows between the jacket's double layers around the breasts. This circulation of warm water dilates the blood vessels and helps to create storage of fat tissue in the breasts.

ANTISEX DEVICES

Sleeping ring This device is attributed to L. B. Sibley of Massachusetts, USA, and was patented in 1856. It was designed specifically to prevent wet dreams. It seems almost cruel to record that it had a number of metal spurs which were meant to prick the penis just enough to awaken the man in order to warn him of 'danger' immediately his organ began to enlarge.

Live wire This is another piece of equipment designed to repress wet dreams and was conceived by E. Roddy of New York in 1917. A small strip, with an electrical circuit joined by wires to a waistbelt, was placed securely into position around the penis. Additional wires ran from the belt to a battery and a bell placed under the bed. An erect penis would cause a surge of electricity to ring the alarm bell, thus awakening the 'owner'.

ROYALTY FACT FILE

Ethelred the Unready, King of England from 978–1016, didn't seem to live up to this name. On his wedding night he was in bed with both his wife AND his mother-in-law!

King Henry VIII, who died on January 1547, is well known for his ultra-active sex life and his six wives. It appears very appropriate that his armour has the largest codpiece on show at the Tower of London.

At the court of King James I (1603–1625) young girls went about bare-breasted as an indication of their virginity.

Anne Boleyn, the second wife of Henry VIII, had three breasts.

Nell Gwyn was the favourite mistress of King Charles II (1660–1685). She was brought up in a brothel and later worked as a barmaid in a similar place.

King William IV (1830–1837) had ten illegitimate children by the actress Dorothy Jordan.

KISSING FACT FILE

Scientists conclude that each passionate kiss uses up to 12 calories.

In 1439, kissing was made illegal in England in a bid to check the spread of diseases through contact.

The Samoans prefer to smell each other rather than kiss.

According to the old custom, a girl who didn't kiss under the mistletoe would be 'barren of children'.

In 1837, a judgment was reached in a European court whereby if a man kissed a woman against her will she was empowered to bite off his nose.

The longest lasting kiss in Hollywood's screen history took place in the 1941 film *You're in the Army Now*. Jane Wyman and Reg Tooney were lips-to-lips for three minutes and five seconds.

It was not until 1978 that the first Indian film kiss was allowed to be seen on screen.

During the 1926 film *Don Juan*, John Barrymore gave a total of 191 kisses to a wide selection of actresses at the rate of one kiss every 53 seconds.

According to the research of the US psychologist Dr Joyce Brothers, the average woman kisses 79 men before she marries.

Kissing in public is a criminal offence in Kuwait.

APHRODISIACS

An aphrodisiac can be defined as a 'drug, food, etc., that excites sexual desire'. Browse through this list of possibilities – who knows what effect, if any, they may have:

Asparagus helps the upkeep of a high energy level.

Caviar coming from a fish, it has been linked to the myth of Aphrodite, the Greek goddess of love born from the foam of the sea.

Oysters Casanova definitely ate lots of them and one must acknowledge his sexual staying power.

Truffles an ancient French proverb cautions: 'Those who have desire to lead virtuous lives should forego truffles'. You have been warned!

Garlic the Greeks and Romans sang its praises and Oriental lovers claimed extra energy after eating it.

Honey very nutritious. Henry VIII ate some every day.

Liquorice French women take a teaspoonful of powdered liquorice in a glass of water.
Pollen helps to maintain the sex drive.

Yohimbine a chemical obtained from the bark of the African tree of the same name. It helps to increase the flow of blood to the genital organs.

Ginseng the Chinese have used it for at least 5000 years and refer to it as the 'elixir of life'. Russian scientists claim that ginseng does increase sexual energy.

Spanish fly **beware** this is lethal. The 'flies' are small, shiny blister-beetles found in Spain and France.

PRIM AND PROPER

In the nineteenth century, makers of Valentine cards dressed Cupid, traditionally naked, in a skirt!

The word 'cock' caused some ultra-modest Victorian Americans to blush with great embarrassment, so the word 'rooster' entered the English language.

In Minnesota it used to be against the law to hang male and female underwear together on the same washing line.

In Victorian times, it was considered improper to have sex on Sunday.

AUTHORS ALL – AND KINKY TOO!

Algernon Charles Swinburne (1837–1909) was a poet who revelled in being whipped by whores in St. John's Wood, London. Another totally bizarre experience he experienced was having sexual relations with a monkey attired as a woman.

Samuel Pepys (1663–1703) is justly famous for his diary. He certainly enjoyed his illicit affairs with his maid and Betty Lane, a linen seller. He was also an avid reader of pornographic material.

Lord Byron (1788–1824), the English poet, had sex with his nanny when he was only 9 years old.

John Ruskin (1819–1900), the noted art critic and author, actually gave up sex on his wedding night! It is said that the sight of his wife's pubic hair so appalled him that he vowed celibacy from that moment on.

SILVER SCREEN FACT FILE

The menstrual cycles of Hollywood's MGM actresses were carefully plotted on charts so that filming schedules could be planned around them.

Errol Flynn had trick chairs in his Hollywood home, which shot out large model penises between the legs of those who sat down.

Cary Grant is said to have had more than 1000 lovers – he has since died.

Hedy Lamarr has said when she was acting in a scene in the film *Ecstasy*, the director stuck a pin in her buttocks in order to obtain a suitable expression akin to orgasm. It was in this 1933 Czech film that she appeared nude.

George Raft, the highly popular screen toughboy, had one principal pleasure — sexual intercourse! For many years he averaged two women each day. On one occasion he had sex with seven beautiful dancers — one after the other — and for 24 hours he was in a state of blissful exhaustion.

Sir Cedric Hardwicke, the distinguished film actor, became impotent. Thereafter, he would introduce himself as 'Sir Seldom Hardprick'.

Jayne Mansfield had sex with Elvis Presley and received an unusual present for her favours — a pink motorcycle.

Tragically, later in her life, Vivien Leigh, the star of the film classic *Gone with the Wind*, went mad while roaming the streets as a pick-up.

Marilyn Monroe used to bleach her pubic hair.

The Japanese were the first to offer soft-porn films for mass audiences.

Belgium is the only country never to have exercised censorship over adult films.

HOLLYWOOD QUOTES

'To succeed with the opposite sex, tell her you're impotent. She can't wait to disprove it.'
Cary Grant, at the age of 72

'Men are those creatures with two legs and eight hands.' *Jayne Mansfield*

'Men are beasts, and even beasts don't behave as they do.' *Brigitte Bardot*

'My dad told me, "Anything is worth waiting for". I waited until I was fifteen.' *Zsa Zsa Gabor*

'Sex appeal is 50% of what you've got and 50% of what people think you've got.' *Sophia Loren*

'Being baldpate is an unfailing sex magnet.' *Telly Savalas*

Asked whether she dressed for men or women: 'I dress for women and undress for men.' *Angie Dickinson*

'Macho does not prove mucho.' *Zsa Zsa Gabor*

'Husbands are chiefly good lovers when they are betraying their wives.' *Marilyn Monroe*

NO WONDER THE ROMAN EMPIRE COLLAPSED

Julius Caesar (100–44 B.C.) — the general and dictator of the Roman Empire who greatly enjoyed satisfying many women. Also, he had pronounced homosexual tendencies. In his early army career, he had a homosexual affair with King Nichomedes of Bithynia in Asia Minor.

Augustus was the first Roman Emperor. Even when he was old, he continued to enjoy deflowering virgins and declared that all Roman widows must remarry because of the declining birthrate.

Tiberius was Emperor from A.D. 14–37 and what a sexual connoisseur he became. On the island of Capri he had expertly tutored young men and women called *spintrae.* They performed sexual gymnastics and executed the sex act in innumerable positions in front of him – all in order to arouse his ardour.

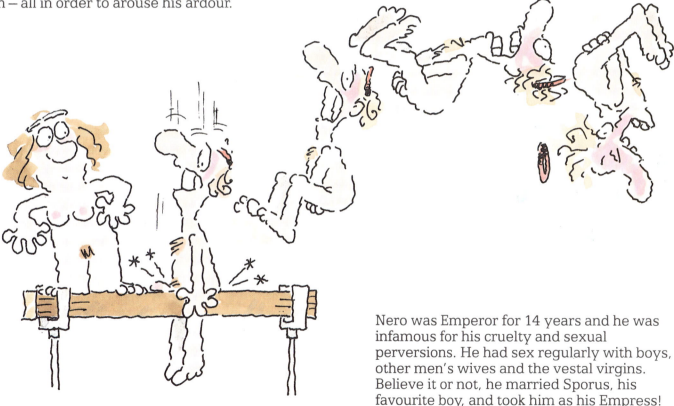

Nero was Emperor for 14 years and he was infamous for his cruelty and sexual perversions. He had sex regularly with boys, other men's wives and the vestal virgins. Believe it or not, he married Sporus, his favourite boy, and took him as his Empress!

MAE WEST – THE BEST

Mae West, who began her career on the American stage but became a big star of the screen, ranked among the world's most sexually attractive women. Maybe her love life can be summed up by her response to a reporter's questions about the writing of her memoirs: 'I do all my best work in bed'. She died in 1980 at the age of 87. Here is a selection of her sayings, which should tell you something about the bawdy, yet good natured, sexy humour of Mae West.

'I used to be Snow White, but I drifted.'

'Give him a free hand and he'll run it all over you.'

'Is that a pistol in your pocket or are you just pleased to see me?'

'A hard man is good to find.'

'It's not the men in my life, but the life in my men that counts.'

When a young man said he was six-feet-seven-inches: 'Never mind the six feet. Let's talk about the seven inches'.

'A curved line is the loveliest distance between two points.'

(On the subject of all-in wrestling) 'If it's all in, why wrestle?

TITTLE TATTLE

In 1973 bottomless waiters were introduced in a Honolulu night club.

A speciality condom, the 'French Tickler', was invented by a Tibetan monk.

In the year 1000 the Chinese custom of footbinding of young girls evolved because tiny feet were the ultimate sex symbol.

Until the 1930s women's underwear was almost exclusively white.

Warren G. Harding, the 29th President of USA (1921–23), used to make love to his mistress in a closet off the Cabinet Room in the White House.

In some parts of Java couples have sex in fields in order to promote crop growth.

The *Kama Sutra*, the Hindu love manual, lists many variations on positions for having sex. The crab, wild boar and bamboo cleft are just three examples.

Marie Stopes (1880–1958) was the English pioneer of birth control. She actually declared that ALL men should wear kilts! Why? Because she believed that the rubbing action of pants or trousers could damage the genitals. It was also rather strange, considering her role in life, that she wasn't aware what masturbation was until she was 29 years old.

San Francisco, claims to be the only city to have a Graduate Schoole of sexology.

Sudanese men reputedly have the largest penises of any race.

In the Dark Ages, following the fall of the Roman Empire, women felt safe from pregnancy if they held a pebble in their hand when making love.

Men and women are the most persistently sexy of all animals.

Ménage à quatre is the French term for sex involving four people.

Penicillin was only discovered as a treatment for VD in 1943.

The term 'blue' as in blue movie or blue material is derived from the blue pencils once used to censor obscene material.

The tune of the US national anthem was once that of a song about a Greek poet who preferred young boys.

The ageing Groucho Marx said he would trade all his fame and fortune for an erection.

Opening brothels catering for foreign diplomats has been one of the CIA's most successful spying methods.

In the 12th century, G. Stalbert advised women to eat bees as a means of birth control.

In the book *Joy of Sex*, an orgasm is described as 'the most religious moment in a person's life'.

Naked City is an American nudist camp located in Indiana.

In 1949 the United Nations launched a campaign for the decriminilisation of prostitution.

'Vatican Roulette' is another term for the rhythm method of birth control.

A 'prickmadam' is... a moss-like herb.

A sceptophiliac is a Peeping Tom.

In Victorian times some women would bathe in fresh strawberries to shrink flabby breasts.

GRAFFITI

Sex is probably the largest single source of all graffiti. It could fill an encyclopedia.

A seven-day honeymoon makes one weak.

An orgasm is a gland finale.

It's hard to be good. IT HAS TO BE HARD TO BE GOOD.

Stick up for your dad – he stuck up for you.

Virginity is like a balloon – one prick and it's gone!

An erection is like Einstein's Theory of Relativity – the more you think about it, the harder it gets.

Sex is like a savings account – after you withdraw you lose interest.

Dudley Moore is a phallic thimble.

Don't be half safe – be cocksure.

A message to all virgins – thanks for nothing.

The devil finds work for idle glands.

COME AGAIN?

Light-hearted sayings often get the point across most easily!

A man has genuinely reached old age when he can't take 'yes' for an answer.

A man who doesn't believe in birth control is called a daddy.

A roll with some honey is a randy man's breakfast.

Perhaps prostitutes keep parrots because they can always do with a cockatoo.

A man should wear a rubber on every conceivable occasion.

OFF THE CHEST

T-Shirts seem to be as popular a medium as graffiti for the glib, double entendre.

Windsurfers do it standing up.

Squash players do it against the wall.

Clergymen do it with reverence.

Astronauts do it in space.

Divers do it underwater.

Ballet dancers do it on their toes.

Anglers do it with rods.

PROVERBIAL FUN

A proverb can be defined as a 'brief, familiar maxim of folk wisdom, usually compressed in form, often involving a bold image...' according to the Longman *Modern English Dictionary.*
The following proverbs might be considered apt even though all are out of context!

Sexual Intercourse
One never loses by doing a good turn.
He who wills the end, wills the means.
There is a good time coming.
Trust helps many both up and down.
Think on the end before you begin.

Illicit affairs and their consequences
He that steals honey should beware of the sting.
Short pleasure, long pain.
He that handles thorns shall prick his finger.
The day obliterates the promise of night.

Birth control
A small leak will sink a big ship.
Thatch your roof before the rain begins.
Prevention is better than cure.

ANIMAL HOUSE

After mating with the queen, the male bee dies and his penis drops off.

Male Mandrills give a red, white and blue display of their colourful genitals.

Snails mate only once in their life, but it can take up to 12 hours for them to complete copulation.

Female moths which are eager to mate, attract males with a strong scent called pheromone, which can be smelled up to 5 miles (8km) away.

The male three-spined stickleback performs an elaborate zig-zag dance to lead the female to the nest. The dance tends to curb his aggression and prepares him for the sexual act.

The male spider picks up a drop of sperm with one leg and inserts it into the female.

The male Adele penguin chooses a mate by rolling a stone towards her feet. If she accepts, they then stand breast to chest and sing a mating song together.

A male African antelope continues to mate until it drops from sheer exhaustion.

Crabs copulate face to face.

Male fireflies produce a 'language' of flashing lights to attract females.

FIVE EMINENTLY SEXUALLY INVOLVED SENIOR CITIZENS

The Duke of Wellington (1769–1852) defeated Napoleon at the Battle of Waterloo in 1815. Just prior to his death at the age of 83 he was enjoying a very full and rewarding love affair with the wife of a politician.

Pablo Picasso (1881–1973), the famous Spanish painter, wasn't too surprised when his wife finally left him in 1963. She complained, quite rightly, that the then 80 year old was cheating on her regularly with other women.

Brigham Young (1801–1877) was the Mormon leader who founded Salt Lake City. When his 27th wife was in the process of divorcing him, she recalled how incensed he was when he was refused sex. He was 72 years old at the time.

Victor Hugo (1802–1885), the French novelist and poet, was having an intense affair with a 27-year-old laundress when he was 70. He wrote in his diary – just six weeks before he died at the age of 80 – of eight most enjoyable sexual encounters.

W. Somerset Maugham (1874–1965), the bisexual author of novels and plays including *Cakes and Ale* and *Of Human Bondage*, confined his sexual activities to men in his later years. When he was 72, he chose 41-year-old Alan Searle to be his secretary, companion and bed partner. Searle said Maugham was the most marvellous lover he'd ever had: 'lusty at 75 and still randy at 84'.

THEY DIED ON THE JOB

Pope Leo VIII acceded to the papacy in A.D. 963. Most embarrassingly, for the Vatican, he died of a stroke whilst committing adultery.

Nelson Rockefeller (1908–1978) was Governor of New York from 1958 until 1973 and Vice-President of the USA for four years. To the end, he thoroughly enjoyed his sex-life and expired whilst copulating with his mistress when he was 71 years old.

Felix Fauré was the President of France for four years from 1895. Whilst performing a sex act with his mistress on a purpose-built sex chair, he suffered a heart attack and died, aged 58 years.

Attila the Hun, although barely 4ft tall (1.2m), was called the 'Scourge of God' when he and his armies overran Europe and terrorised the crumbling Roman Empire. He died making love to his wife in A.D. 453.

QUICK QUIZ

1 In 1974, 1200 naked people set the record for which craze?

2 In what situation do most girls lose their viginity?

3 Which US president said: 'I have committed adultery in my heart many times'?

4 What did Aldous Huxley call 'the most unnatural of sexual perversions'?

5 What were set up in Iowa City, USA, and Tokyo, Japan, in 1964?

6 Are the odds for or against a married woman having an affair?

7 Which is the most effective oral contraceptive?

8 What is peculiar about the average pair of women's breasts?

9 Which US President was quoted as saying, 'I'm never through with a girl until I've had her three ways'?

10 Who is a 'cuckold'?

ANSWERS TO QUICK QUIZ

1 Streaking 2 In a motor car 3 Jimmy Carter 4 Chastity 5 Sperm Banks 6 Against 3.5 to 1 7 To say 'no' 8 One breast is larger than the other 9 J. F. Kennedy 10 A husband whose wife has taken a lover.

Mike Gordon himself escaped from formal schooling in Lancashire after being caned for decorating the school toilets and tattooing his classmates. Frustratingly, his refuge at Rochdale Art College was curtailed by a father who insisted that his son pursue the more robust trade of plumbing. Yet his talent for humorous illustration triumphed; moving to Sussex, he became a professional illustrator in 1983 through the encouragement of his wife and the need to feed four children. An active but mildly confused life consists of Christmas spent designing Easter cards and the rest of the year juggling his deadlines on a staggeringly wide range of book illustration. With well over 50 titles credited to his pen and brush to date, Mike was the "Berol Cartoonist of the Year" in 1988 and runner-up as the international cartoonist in Italy's "Trento Fra Realto e Follia".

David Smith is a former teacher who works from his Cheshire study, the shelves of which are filled with many of the 200 or so books with which he has been involved over the last twenty years. From educational text books, he moved on to illustrated information titles, picture dictionaries and puzzle books. Also a syndicated newspaper writer, he has been working in tandem with Mike Gordon recently on a wide range of children's books as well as fact-filled illustrated works and humour titles. His ability to amass facts in a lighthearted manner is admirably suited to the world's favourite topic and to Mike's amusing and pertinent visual interpretation.

First published in the UK 1989 by Firebird Books
P.O. Box 327, Poole, Dorset BH15 2RG

Copyright © 1989 Firebird Books Ltd
Text copyright © 1989 David Smith
Illustrations copyright © 1989 Mike Gordon

Distributed in Australia by
The Five Mile Press, 379 Smith Street
P.O. Box 356, Fitzroy, Victoria 3065

British Library Cataloguing in Publication Data
Smith, David
  Phallic thimbles: the illustrated guide to sexual trivia.
  1. Sex relations
  I. Title II. Gordon, Mike
  306.7
  ISBN 1 85134 146 1

All rights reserved. No part of this book may be reproduced or transmitted in any form or by any means, electronic or mechanical, including photocopying, recording or any information storage and retrieval system, without permission in writing from the Publisher.

Typeset by Bournetype, Bournemouth
Printed and bound in Great Britain by Maclehose & Partners Ltd, Portsmouth